Edmund Goldsmid, Charles Kirkpatrick Sharpe

A Ballad Book

Popular and Romantic Ballads and Congs current in Annandale and other

Parts of Scotland Vol. 1

Edmund Goldsmid, Charles Kirkpatrick Sharpe

A Ballad Book
Popular and Romantic Ballads and Congs current in Annandale and other Parts of Scotland Vol. 1

ISBN/EAN: 9783744774536

Printed in Europe, USA, Canada, Australia, Japan

Cover: Foto ©Thomas Meinert / pixelio.de

More available books at **www.hansebooks.com**

Bibliotheca Curiosa.

A
BALLAD BOOK;

OR,

POPULAR AND ROMANTIC BALLADS AND
SONGS CURRENT IN ANNANDALE AND
OTHER PARTS OF SCOTLAND.

COLLECTED BY

CHARLES KIRKPATRICK SHARPE.

Reprinted from the Rare Original Edition of 1824,

and Edited by

EDMUND GOLDSMID.

PART I.

PRIVATELY PRINTED, EDINBURGH

1891.

INTRODUCTION.

THE collection of Ballads here reprinted is well known by name to all lovers of this class of Ancient Poetry, but the book itself can have been seen by few. Privately printed in 1824 for distribution among the Editor's friends, only thirty copies issued from the press, and, of these, half at least have found a permanent resting-place on the shelves of our large public or semi-public Libraries.*

The Editor was one of a band of quaint Antiquarian *Littérateurs*, which included Maidment,† Kinloch,‡ Buchan,§ &c., who devoted much time and labour to rescuing these unwritten traditions of the land, at the very period when they were sinking into oblivion. Gathered, as he tells us, from the mouths of nurses, wet and dry, dairy-

---

* A copy fetched £6 17s. 6d. at Mr. J. Maidment's sale.

† Editor of "A New Book of Old Ballads," "A North Countrie Garland," &c., &c.

‡ Editor of "The Ballad Book."

§ Editor of "Ancient Ballads and Songs of the North of Scotland."

maids, and tenants' daughters, it is not surprising
if in form they are often rough and uncouth, and
in ideas not always over-delicate. But, notwith-
standing all their faults, nay, for that very reason,
they will not fail to interest all who yet value

> The songs, to savage virtue dear,
> That won of yore the public ear,
> Ere polity, sedate and sa*e,
> Had quench'd the fires of Feudal rage.

"Give me the writing of the Ballads, and you
may make the Laws," cried Fletcher of Saltoun,
and he was right. Alfred for generations pro-
bably owed as much of his fame to the Ballads he
wrote* as to the laws he "adapted," to use our
modern dramatic expression, from Ethelbert, Ina,
or Offa. The minstrel has been in turn protected
by Edward of York and treated as a rogue and a
vagabond by his illustrious great grand-daughter;†
Richard Cœur-de-Lion is perhaps better known
as a Troubadour than as the Conqueror of Cyprus;
generation after generation of our peasantry have
cheered the long winter evenings, and listened with
awe to the tale of Rothiemay, or the fate of
"Fause Sir John"; Governments have quaked
at the sound of "Lilliburlero," or "Ça ira."

* William of Malmesbury's Chronicles.
† Viner's "General Abridgment of the Laws of
England."

In "A Ballad Book," at least five ballads were printed for the first time, viz.—

> Lady Dysmal.
> Glasgow Peggie.
> Fair Margaret of Craignargat.
> O Errol it's a bonny place.
> Ritchie Storie.

I have printed Mr. Sharpe's book word for word, only altering the position of his notes from the beginning to the end of each Ballad ; * giving a name to such Ballads as had had none assigned them ; adding a Table of Contents ; and, lastly, subjoining such notes as seemed to me *really* necessary. I have always held that too many notes impede rather than help the reader, and I have acted in accordance with my opinion.

EDMUND GOLDSMID.

EDINBURGH, *Oct.* 12*th*, 1883.

---

* The *original* notes are distinguished throughout by the initials *C.K.S.*

ORIGINAL PREFACE.

COURTEOUS READER,

As this book, of which only thirty copies are printed, shall cost thee nothing, save a little time thrown away on its perusal, which most Antiquaries can very well spare, I will make no apology to thee for the compiling of it. The truth is, I was anxious after this fashion, to preserve a few songs that afforded me much delight in my early youth, and are not to be found at all, or complete, or in the same shape in other Collections. These have been mostly gathered from the mouths of nurses, wet and dry, singing to their babes and sucklings, dairy-maids pursuing their vocation in the cow-house, and tenants' daughters, while giving the Lady (as every Laird's wife was once called) a spinning day, whilom an anniversary tribute in Annandale. Several, too, were picked up from tailors, who were wont to reside in my father's castle, while misshaping clothes for the children and servants. Though I am sensible that none of these Ballads are of much merit, I regret that my memory doth not now serve me as to many more, the outlines of which alone I remember. Some, indeed, I have suppressed on account of their grossness; confessing, at the same time, that several here printed are not over delicate; but little will be found to corrupt the imagination, and nothing to inflame the passions. Sufficit! I have inserted a few from MS. Collections in my possession, and perhaps shall be tempted by and by to add a second volume from the same sources. In the meantime, gentle reader,

HAIL! AND FAREWELL!

INDEX TO PART I.

A BALLAD BOOK.

I.

FAIR JANET.*

"YE maun gang to your father, Janet,
   Ye maun gang to him soon ;
Ye maun gang to your father, Janet,
   In case that his days are dune !"

Janet's awa' to her father,
   As fast as she could hie ;
"O, what's your will wi' me, father ?
   O, what's your will wi' me ?"

"My will wi' you, fair Janet," he said,
   "It is both bed and board ;
Some say that ye lo'e sweet Willie,
   But ye maun wed a French lord."

---

* This ballad, the subject of which appears to have been
very popular, is printed as it was sung by an old woman in
Perthshire. The air is extremely beautiful.—C. K. S. It
is usually printed under the title of "Willie and Annet,"
and was also published by Mr. Finlay in an improved (?)
version, under the title of "Sweet Willie."

"A French lord maun I wed, father?
A French lord maun I wed?
Then by my sooth," quo fair Janet,
  "He's neer enter my bed."

Janet's awa' to her chamber,
  As fast as she could go ;
Wha's the first ane that tapped there,
  But sweet Willie, her jo?

"O we maun part this love, Willie,
  That has been lang between ;
There's a French lord coming o'er the sea,
  To wed me wi' a ring ;
There's a French lord coming o'er the sea,
  To wed and tak' me hame."

"If we maun part this love, Janet,
  It causeth mickle woe ;
If we maun part this love, Janet,
  It makes me into mourning go."

"But ye maun gang to your three sisters,
  Meg, Marion, and Jean ;
Tell them to come to fair Janet,
  In case that her days are dune."

Willie's awa' to his three sisters,
  Meg, Marion and Jean ;
"O, haste and gang to fair Janet,
  I fear that her days are dune."

Some drew to them their silken hose,
  Some drew to them their shoon,
Some drew to them their silk manteils,
  Their coverings to put on ;
And they're awa' to fair Janet,
  By the hie light o' the moon.

*   *   *   *   *

" O, I have born this babe, Willie,
  Wi' muckle toil and pain ;
Take hame, take hame your babe, Willie,
  For nurse I dare be nane."

He's tane his young son in his arms,
  And kiss't him cheek and chin—
And he's awa' to his mother's bower,
  By the hie light o' the moon.

"O, open, open, mother," he says,
  "O, open, and let me in ;
The rain rains on my yellow hair,
  And the dewdrops o'er my chin—
And I hae my young son in my arms,
  I fear that his days are dune."

With her fingers lang and sma',
  She lifted up the pin ;
And with her arms lang and sma',
  Received the baby in.

"Gae back, gae back, now sweet Willie,
　And comfort your fair lady ;
For where ye had but ae nourice,
　Your young son shall hae three."

Willie he was scarce awa'
　And the lady put to bed,
When in and came her father dear,
　"Make haste and busk the bride."

"There's a sair pain in my head, father,
　There's a sair pain in my side,
And ill, O ill, am I, father,
　This day for to be a bride.

"O, ye maun busk this bonny bride,
　And put a gay mantle on ;
For she shall wed this auld French lord,
　Gin she should die the morn."

Some pat on the gay green robes,
　And some pat on the brown,
But Janet put on the scarlet robes
　To shine foremost throw the town.

And some they mounted the black steed,
　And some mounted the brown,
But Janet mounted the milk-white steed
　To ride foremost throw the town.

"O, wha will guide your horse, Janet?
  O, wha will guide him best?"
"O, wha but Willie, my true love,
  He kens I lo'e him best!"

And whan they came to Marie's kirk,
  To tye the haly ban,
Fair Janet's cheek looked pale and wan,
  And her colour gaed an cam.

When dinner it was past and done,
  And dancing to begin;
"O, we'll go take the bride's maidens,
  And we'll go fill the ring."

O, ben than cam' the auld French lord,
  Saying, "Bride, will ye dance wi' me?"
"Awa', awa', ye auld French lord,
  Your face I downa see."

O, ben than cam' now sweet Willie,
  He cam' with ane advance;
"O, I'll go tak' the bride's maidens,
  And we'll go tak' a dance."

"I've seen ither days wi' you, Willie,
  And so has mony mae;
Ye would hae dance wi' me mysel',
  Let a' my maidens gae."

O, ben then cam' now sweet Willie,
   Saying, " Bride, will ye dance wi' me?"
" Aye, by my sooth, and that I will,
   Gin my back should break in three."

She had nae turned her throw the dance,
   Throw the dance but thrice,
Whan she fell doun at Willie's feet,
   And up did never rise !

Willie's ta'en the key of his coffer,
   And gi'en it to his man,
"Gae hame, and tell my mother dear,
   My horse he has me slain ;
Bid her be kind to my young son,
   For father he has nane."

The tane was buried in Marie's kirk
   And the tither in Marie's quier ;
Out of the tane there grew a birk,
   And the tither a bonny brier.

II.

THE LASSES O' THE CANNOGATE.*

The lasses o' the Cannogate, †
O' they are wondrous nice,
They winna gie a single kiss
But for a double price.

Gar hang them, gar hang them,
Heich upon a tree,
For we'll get better up the gate
For a bawbee.

III.

THE VAIN GUDEWIFE.

I'll gar our gudeman trow
That I'll sell the ladle,
If he winna buy to me
A new side saddle
To ride to the kirk, and frae the kirk,
And round about the toun,—
Stand about, ye fisher jads,
And gie my goun room !

---

* The two following songs were remembered thirty years ago by an old gentlewoman. The first seems to be a satire on the Court ladies of Edinburgh.—C. K. S.

† A street in the old town of Edinburgh, a continuation of the High Street. It was once the fashionable quarter of the town.

I'il gar our gudeman trow
　That I'll tak' the fling strings,
If he winna buy to me
　Twelve bonnie goud rings,—
Ane for ilka finger,
　And twa for ilka thoom,—
Stand about, ye fisher jads,
　And gie my goun room!

I'll gar our gudeman trow
　That I'll tak' the glengore,
If he winna fee to me
　Three valets or four,
To beir my tail up frae the dirt,
　And ush me throw the toun,—
Stand about, ye fisher jads,
　And gie my goun room!*

IV.

LADY DYSMAL.

THERE was a king, and a glorious king,
　And a king of mickle fame;
And he had daughters only one,
　Lady Dysmal was her name.

---

* As illustrations of the above song, *vide* Sir Richard
Maitland's Poems, beginning :—
　　" Some wyfis of the Borroustoun
　　　So wander vane are, and wantoun."
And also Sir David Lindsay's supplication against Syde
Taillis and Mussalit Faces.—C. K. S.

He had a boy, and a kitchen boy,
  A boy of mickle scorn ;
And she lov'd him lang, and she lov'd him
    aye,
  Till the grass o'ergrew the corn.

When twenty weeks were gone and past,
  O, she began to greet ;
Her petticoats grew short before,
  And her stays they wadna meet.

It fell upon a winter's night,
  The king could get nae rest ;
He cam unto his daughter dear,
  Just like a wand'ring ghaist.

He cam into her bed-chamber,
  And drew the curtains round,—
" What aileth thee, my daughter dear ?
  I fear you've gotten wrong."

"O, if I have, despise me not,
  For he is all my joy ;
I will forsake baith dukes and earls,
  And marry your kitchen boy."

"Go call to me my merry men all,
  By thirty and by three ;
Go call to me my kitchen boy,
  We'll murder him secretlie."

There was nae din that could be heard,
　　And ne'er a word was said,
Till they got him baith fast and sure,
　　Between twa feather beds.

" Go, cut the heart out of his breast,
　　And put it in a cup of gold ;
And present it to his Dysmal dear,
　　For she is baith stout and bold."

They've cut the heart out of his breast,
　　And put it in a cup of gold ;
And presented it to his Dysmal dear,
　　Who was baith stout and bold.

"O, come to me, my hinney, my heart,
　　O, come to me, my joy ;
O, come to me, my hinney, my heart,
　　My father's kitchen boy."

She's ta'en the cup out of their hands,
　　And set it at her bed head ;
She wash'd it wi' the tears that fell from her
　　eyes,
　　And next morning she was dead.

" O, where were ye, my merry men all,
　　Whom I paid meat and wage,
Ye didna hold my cruel hand,
　　When I was in my rage ? "

" For gone is a' my heart's delight,
    And gone is a' my joy ;
For my dear Dysmal she is dead,
    And so is my kitchen boy." *

V.

THE BRIDEGROOM.

THERE lived a man into the west,
    And O ! but he was cruel ;
Upon his waddin' nicht at e'en,
    He sat up and grat for gruel.

They brought to him a good sheep's head,
    A napkin, and a towel,—
" Gae tak' your whim-whams a' frae me,
    And bring me fast my gruel."

---

* This stupid ballad, printed as it was sung in Annandale, is founded on the well-known story of the Prince of Salerno's daughter; but with what uncouth change! Dysmal for Ghismonda, and Guiscardo transformed into a greasy kitchen boy :

    " An ounce of civet, good apothecary,
        To sweeten my imagination."

The reader will immediately remember Hogarth's picture and Churchill's exclamation :—

    " Poor Sigismunda, what a fate was thine !"—C. K. S.

Compare also the "Story of a Lover's Heart" in Disraeli's " Curiosities of Literature."

The BRIDE *speaks.*

" There is nae meal into the hous,
 What shall I do, my jewel?"
" Gae to the pock and shake a lock,
 For I canna want my gruel."

" There is nae milk into the hous,
 What shall I do, my jewel?"
" Gae to the midden and milk the soo,
 For I wunna want my gruel." *

VI.

MARIE HAMILTON.

WORD'S gane to the kitchen
 And word's gane to the ha',
That Marie Hamilton gangs wi' bairn
 To the hichest Stewart of a'.

He's courted her in the kitchen,
 He's courted her in the ha',
He's courted her in the laigh cellar,
 And that was the warst of a'!

---

* This song, from some original words of the air to which
Auld Robin Gray was latterly adapted, appears to have
been composed on a similar melancholy event.
" The bridegroom grat when the sun gaed down (*Repeat*)
And ' Och,' quo' he, ' It's come o'er soon,' " &c.—C. K. S.

She's tyed it in her apron,
   And she's thrown it in the sea,
Says "Sink ye, swim ye, bonny wee be'
   You'l ne'er get mair o' me."

Down then cam' the auld Queen,
   Goud tassels tying her hair,
"O, Marie, where's the bonny wee babe,
   That I heard greet sae sair?"

"There was never a babe intill my room,
   As little designs to be;
It was but a touch o' my sair side,
   Come o'er my fair bodie."

"O, Marie, put on your robes o' black,
   Or else your robes o' brown,
For ye maun gang wi' me the night,
   To see fair Edinbro' town."

"I winna put on my robes o' black,
   Nor yet my robes o' brown,
But I'll put on my robes o' white,
   To shine through Edinbro' town."

When she gaed up the Cannogate,
   She laugh'd loud laughters three;
But whan she cam down the Cannogate,
   The tears blinded her e'e.

When she gaed up the Parliament stair,
  The heel cam aff her shee,
And lang or she cam down again,
  She was condemn'd to dee.

When she cam down the Cannogate,
  The Cannogate sae free,
Mony a ladie look'd o'er her window,
  Weeping for this ladie.

"Ye need nae weep for me," she says,
  "Ye need nae weep for me,
For had I not slain mine own sweet babe,
  This death I wadna dee.

"Bring me a bottle of wine," she says,
  "The best that e'er ye hae,
That I may drink to my weil wishers,
  And they may drink to me.

"Here's a health to the jolly sailors,
  That sail upon the main,
Let them never let on to my father and
    mother,
  But what I'm coming hame.

"Here's a health to the jolly sailors
  That sail upon the sea;
Let them never let on to my father and
    mother,
  That I am here to dee.

"Oh, little did my mother think,
    The day she cradled me,
What lands I was to travel through,
    What death I was to dee.

"Oh, little did my father think,
    The day he held up me,
What lands I was to travel through,
    What death I was to dee.

"Last night I wash'd the Queen's feet,
    And gently laid her down ;
And a' the thanks I've gotten the nicht,
    To be hang'd in Edinbro' town.

"Last nicht there was four Maries,
    The nicht there'l be but three ;
There was Marie Seton, and Marie Beton,
    And Marie Carmichael, and me." *

---

* In the Border Minstrelsy (vol. iii. page 87) is a much more refined edition of this ballad, which is supposed to relate the misadventure of one of Queen Marie's ladies. It is singular that during the reign of the Czar Peter, one of his Empress's attendants, a Miss Hamilton (spelt Hambleton by Sir Walter Scott), was executed for the murder of a natural child,—not her first crime in that way, as was suspected ; and the Czar, whose admiration of her beauty did not preserve her life, stood upon the scaffold till her head was struck off, which he lifted by the ear, and kissed on the lips. I cannot help thinking that the two stories have been confused in the ballad, for if Marie Hamilton was executed in Scotland, it is not likely that her relations

VII.

LADY DUNDONALD.

WEEL it becomes the Lady Dundonald,
  To sit liltin' at her rock,
And weel it becomes the Laird of Dundonald,
  To wear his hodden gray frock !
    Chorus.—Lilty eery, lardy lardy
      Lilty eery, lardy lam.

(*Enter* MARG'ET.)
" My Lady, there is a lass at the door wants to be
    feed."
" What fee does she want ? "   " Five punds."
" Five punds is o'er mony punds, to be
  Drawing out the tail o' a rock."
    Chorus.—Lilty, eery, &c.

" Tell her I will gee her four punds,
  And spin a' the backs mysel."
    Chorus.—Lilty, eery, &c.

resided beyond seas, and we have no proof that Hamilton
was really the name of the woman who made a slip with
Darnley.—C. K. S. A third version is given by Motherwell,
as the one current in the west of Scotland (page 401); but
the most complete is that reprinted by the Aungervyle
Society (series 1, 1881). In Knox's " History of the Re-
formation " (page 373-4), it is stated that the murderess was
a Frenchwoman in the Queen's suite, and the father of the
child the Queen's apothecary. " This was the beginning
of the regiment of Mary, Queen of Scots, and these were
the fruits which she brought forth of France," exclaims the
bigoted Scotsman, with admirable love of justice !

(*Enter* MARG'ET.)
" My Lady, what will I tell you noo,
   Isna our kitchen lass wi' bairn !
What may that be till?
   The Laird, I needna speir."
     Chorus.—Lilty eery, &c.

" He has fifteen at the fireside **else,**
And that will mak sixteen,
And sae it will een ;
It was me that made him a Laird ;
And deel speed sic Lairds ! "
     Chorus.—Lilty eery, &c.

" Hear, Marg'et."   " What does my Lady want
       noo?"
" Bring ben the brandy bottle, your waas,
And tak' a dram yoursel',
And gar we tak' twa."
     Chorus.—Lilty eery, &c.

" I think we may as weel
Tak' our ain geer oursels,
For it is gaein' whether or no."
     Chorus.—Lilty eery, &c.

(*Enter* JOHN.)
" My Lady, there is company come."
" Fashious fock, John; I want nae company,
I am spinning at my rock."
     Chorus.—Lilty eery, &c.

" My Lady, the servants is going to their beds,
They want the doup of a candle."
" Tell them to put doups and doups thegither,
And that will gie them licht." *
  Chorus.—Lilty eery, &c.

VIII.

JENNY.

JENNY, scho's ta'en a deep surprise,
 And scho's spew'd a' her crowdie,
Her minnie scho ran to seek her a dram,
 But scho stude mair need o' the howdie.

" O, Sandie, dinna ye mind," quo' scho,
 " Whan ye gart me drink the brandy,
Whan ye yerkit me ow'r amang the braume,
 And plaid me Houghmagandy ! "

---

* This strange folly was generally sung by a man, with a woman's cap on his head, a distaff, and a spindle. The dialogue, of which the subjoined is only a fragment, was chanted in recitative. Can this song possibly allude to Elizabeth, daughter and heiress of William Cochrane of Cochrane, who married Alexander, a younger son of John Blair of Blair? Her father made a settlement of his estate in her favour 1593. At Gosford, a seat of the Earl of Wemyss, is a full-length portrait of a hideous old woman, with her spinning implements, and a starved cat, said to be the Lady Dundonald of the ballad, but to me it appears to be the figure of a Flemish peasant.—C. K. S.

IX.

DESERTED.

AND sae ye've treated me,
And sae ye've treated me ;
I'll never lo'e anither man,
Sae weil as I've lo'ed thee.
And sae ye've treated me,
And sae ye've treated me ;
The deil pit on your windin' sheet
Three hours before you dee !

X.

THE TWA SISTERS.

THERE liv'd twa sisters in a bower,
  Hey Edinbruch, how Edinbruch,
There liv'd twa sisters in a bower,
    Stirling for aye ;
The youngest o' them, O, she was a flower !
  Bonny Sanct Johnstoune that stands upon Tay.

There cam a squire frae the west,
  Hey Edinbruch, how Edinbruch,
There cam a squire frae the west,
    Stirling for aye ;
He lo'ed them baith, but the youngest best,
  Bonny Sanct Johnstoune that stands upon Tay.

He gied the eldest a gay gold ring,
    Hey Edinbruch, how Edinbruch,
He gied the eldest a gay gold ring,
    Stirling for aye ;
But he lo'ed the youngest aboon a' thing,
    Bonny Sanct Johnstoune that stands upon Tay.

"Oh, sister, sister, will ye go to the sea?
    Hey Edinbruch, how Edinbruch,
Oh, sister, sister, will ye go to the sea?
    Stirling for aye ;
Our father's ships sail bonnilie,
    Bonny Sanct Johnstoune that stands upon Tay."

The youngest sat down upon a stane,
    Hey Edinbruch, how Edinbruch,
The youngest sat down upon a stane,
    Stirling for aye ;
The eldest shot the youngest in,
    Bonny Sanct Johnstoune that stands upon Tay.

"Oh, sister, sister, lend me your hand,
    Hey Edinbruch, how Edinbruch,
Oh, sister, sister, lend me your hand,
    Stirling for aye ;
And you shall hae my gouden fan,
    Bonny Sanct Johnstoune that stands upon Tay.

"Oh, sister, sister, save my life,
    Hey Edinbruch, how Edinbruch,

Oh, sister, sister, save my life,
  Stirling for aye ;
And ye shall be the squire's wife,
  Bonny Sanct Johnstoune that stands upon Tay."

First she sank, and then she swam,
  Hey Edinbruch, how Edinbruch,
First she sank, and then she swam,
  Stirling for aye ;
Until she cam to Tweed mill dam,
  Bonny Sanct Johnstoune that stands upon Tay.

The millar's daughter was baking bread,
  Hey Edinbruch, how Edinbruch,
The millar's daughter was baking bread,
  Stirling for aye.
She went for water, as she had need,
  Bonny Sanct Johnstoune that stands upon Tay.

"Oh, father, father, in our mill dam,
  Hey Edinbruch, how Edinbruch,
Oh, father, father, in our mill dam,
  Stirling for aye ;
There's either a lady, or a milk-white swan,
  Bonny Sanct Johnstoune that stands upon Tay."

They could nae see her fingers small,
  Hey Edinbruch, how Edinbruch,
They could nae see her fingers small,
  Stirling for aye ;

c

Wi' diamond rings they were cover'd all,
  Bonny Sanct Johnstoune that stands upon Tay.

They could nae see her yellow hair,
  Hey Edinbruch, how Edinbruch,
They could nae see her yellow hair,
    Stirling for aye ;
Sae mony knotts and platts war there,
  Bonny Sanct Johnstoune that stands upon Tay.

They could nae see her lily feet,
  Hey Edinbruch, how Edinbruch,
They could nae see her lilly feet,
    Stirling for aye ;
Her gowden fringes war sae deep,
  Bonny Sanct Johnstoune that stands upon Tay.

Bye there cam a fiddler fair,
  Hey Edinbruch, how Edinbruch,
Bye there cam a fiddler fair,
    Stirling for aye ;
And he's taen three taits o' her yellow hair,
  Bonny Sanct Johnstoune that stands upon Tay.*

    *   *   *   *   *

---

   * Various sets of this song have been printed. It was popular both in England and Scotland. The air is beautiful.—C.K.S.

   It is usually called "Binnorie," from the ordinary chorus. A version is given in the Border Minstrelsy, which is far more complete. A parody of it is to be found in D'Urfey's, "Pills to purge Melancholy."

XI.
THE FIDDLER'S BENISON.

My blessing gae wi' ye, Jock Rob, Jock Rob,
My blessing gae wi' you, Jock Rob;
For whan ye come here, ye mak' us good cheer,
And gar our blythe bottoms play bob!

XII.
THE SOUTAR AND THE SOO.

THE soutar gied the soo a kiss—
"Grumph," quo' scho, "it's for my briss."
"And whare gat ye sae sweet a mou?"
Quo' the soutar to the soo.
"Grumph," quo' scho, "and whare gat ye
A tongue sae sleekie and sae slee?" *

XIII.
GLENLOGIE.

Four and twenty nobles sits in the king's ha',
Bonnie Glenlogie is the flower among them a'.

In came Lady Jean skipping on the floor,
And she has chosen Glenlogie 'mong a' that was
      there.

---

* It is very strange, as well as amusing, to observe how
much our ancient poets detested soutars. Examples are
too numerous to be quoted.—C. K. S.

She turned to his footman, and thus she did say :
"Oh, what is his name, and where does he stay?"

"His name is Glenlogie, when he is from home,
He is of the gay Gordons, his name it is John."

"Glenlogie, Glenlogie, an' you will prove kind,
My love is laid on you, I am telling my mind."

He turned about lightly, as the Gordons does a',
"I thank you, Lady Jean, my love is promised
awa'."

She called on her maidens her bed for to make,
Her rings and her jewels all from her to take.

In came Jeanie's father, a wae man was he,
Says, "I'll wed you to Drumfendrich, he has mair
gold than he."

Her father's own chaplain, being a man of great
skill,
He wrote him a letter, and indited it well;

The first lines he looked at, a light laugh laughed
he,
But ere he read through it, the tears blinded his
e'e.

Oh, pale and wan looked she when Glenlogie cam'
in,
But even rosy grew she when Glenlogie sat down.

"Turn round, Jeanie Melville, turn round to this
side,
And I'll be the bridegroom, and you'll be the
bride."

Oh, 'twas a merry wedding, and the portion down
told,
Oh, bonnie Jeanie Melville, who was scarce six-
teen years old.*

XIV.
DICKIE MACPHALION.

I WENT to the mill, but the miller was gone,
I sat me down, and cried ochone !
To think on the days that are past and gone
Of Dickie Macphalion that's slain,
    Shoo, shoo, shoolaroo,
To think on the days that are past and gone,
Of Dickie Macphalion that's slain.

---

* This ballad was first printed in "The Scottish Min-
strel," vol. iv., 1822. The version there given differs con-
siderably from this. An "expurgated" text was printed
in "The Popular Rhymes of Scotland" in 1826, and,
mirabile dictu, is there said to be "printed for the *first*
time."

I sold my rock, I sold my reel,
And sae hae I my spinning wheel,
And a' to buy a cap of steel
For Dickie Macphalion that's slain!
    Shoo, shoo, shoolaroo,
And a' to buy a cap of steel
For Dickie Macphalion that's slain.*

XV.

GLASGOW PEGGIE.

As I cam' in by Glasgow town,
The Highland troops were a' before me,
And the bonniest lass that e'er I saw,
She lives in Glasgow, they ca' her Peggie.

I wad gie my bonnie black horse,
So wad I my gude grey naigie,
If I were twa hundred miles in the north,
And nane wi' me but my bonnie Peggie!"

Up then spak' her father dear,
Dear wow! but he was wondrous sorrie—
"Weel may ye steal a cow or a yowe,
But ye dare nae steal my bonnie Peggie."

Up then spak her mother dear,
Dear wow! but she spak' wondrous sorrie—
"Now since I have brought ye up this length,
Wad ye gang awa' wi' a Highland fellow?"

---

* A Ballad of evidently Irish origin.

He set her on his bonnie black horse,
He set himself on his gude grey naigie ;
And they have ridden o'er hills and dales,
And he's awa' wi' his bonnie Peggie.

They have ridden o'er hills and dales,
They have ridden o'er mountains many,
Until they cam' to a low, low glen,
And there he's lain down wi' his bonnie Peggie.

Up then spak' the Earl of Argyle,
Dear wow ! but he spak' wondrous sorrie—
"The bonniest lass in a' Scotland,
Is off and awa' wi' a Highland fellow."

Their bed was of the bonnie green grass,
Their blankets war o' the hay sae bonnie ;
He folded his philabeg below her head,
And he's lain down wi' his bonnie Peggie.

Up then spak' the bonnie Lowland lass,
And wow ! but she spak' wondrous sorrie—
"I'se warrant my mither wad hae a gay sair
    heart
To see me lien' here wi' you, my Willie."

"In my father's house there's feather beds,
Feather beds, and blankets mony ;
They're a' mine, and they'll sune be thine,
And what needs your mither be sae sorrie,
    Peggie ?

"Dinna you see yon nine score o' kye,
Feeding on yon hill sae bonnie?
There a' mine, and they'll sune be thine,
And what needs your mither be sorrie, Peggie?

"Dinna ye see yon nine score o' sheep,
Feeding on yon brae sae bonnie?
They're a' mine, and they'll sune be thine,
And what needs your mither be sorrie for ye?

"Dinna ye see yon bonnie white house,
Shining on yon brae sae bonnie?
And I am the Earl of the Isle of Skye,
And surely my Peggie will be ca'd a lady."*

XVI.
TAM O' THE LIN.

TAM O' LIN's daughter scho sat on the stair,
And, "Wow," quo scho, "Father, am na I fair?
There's mony ane wed wi' an unwhiter skin"—
"The deil whorl 't off," quo Tam o' the Lin.

Tam o' Lin's daughter scho sat on the brig,
And, "Wow," quo scho, "Father, am na I trig?"
The brig it brak', and she tummel'd in—
"Your tocher's paid," quo Tam o' the Lin.

---

* This ballad is better known under the title of the "Ear
of Hume," or the "Banks of Omey."

XVII.

MAY COLLIN.

OH, heard ye of a bloody knight,
　　Lived in the south country?
For he has betrayed eight ladies fair,
　　And drowned them in the sea.

Then next he went to May Collin,
　　She was her father's heir;
The greatest beauty in the land,
　　I solemnly declare.

"I am a knight of wealth and might,
　　Of townlands twenty-three;
And you'll be the lady of them all
　　If you will go with me."

"Excuse me, then, Sir John," she says,
　　"To wed I am too young—
Without I have my parents' leave,
　　With you I darena gang."

"Your parents' leave you soon shall have,
　　In that they will agree;
For I have made a solemn vow
　　This night you'll go with me."

From below his arm he pulled a charm,
  And stuck it in her sleeve ;
And he has made her go with him,
  Without her parents' leave.

Of gold and silver she has got
  With her twelve hundred pound ;
And the swiftest steed her father had
  She has ta'en to ride upon.

So privily they went along,
  They made no stop or stay,
Till they came to the fatal place,
  That they call Bunion Bay.

It being in a lonely place,
  And no house there was nigh,
The fatal rocks were long and steep,
  And none could hear her cry.

"Light down," he said, "fair May Collin,
  Light down, and speak with me,
For here I've drowned eight ladies fair,
  And the ninth one you shall be."

"Is this your bowers and lofty towers,
  So beautiful and gay,
Or is it for my gold," she said,
  "You take my life away?"

"Strip off," he says, "thy jewels fine,
 So costly and so brave,
For they are too costly and too fine
 To throw in the sea wave."

"Take all I have my life to save,
 Oh, good Sir John, I pray,
Let it ne'er be said you killed a maid,
 Upon her wedding-day."

"Strip off," he says, "thy holland smock,
 "That's bordered with the lawn,
For it's too costly and too fine
 To rot on the sea sand."

"Oh, turn about, Sir John," she said,
 Your back about to me ;
For it never was comely for a man
 A naked woman to see."

But as he turned him round about,
 She threw him in the sea,
Saying, "Lie you there, you false Sir John,
 Where you thought to lay me.

"Oh, lie you there, you traitor false,
 Where you thought to lay me ;
For though you stripped me to the skin,
 Your clothes you've got with thee."

Her jewels fine she did put on,
　　So costly, rich, and brave,
And then with speed she mounts his steed,
　　So well she did behave.

That lady fair being void of fear,
　　Her steed being swift and free,
And she has reached her father's gate
　　Before the clock struck three.

Then first she called her stable groom,
　　He was her waiting man ;
Soon as he heard his lady's voice,
　　He stood with cap in hand.

"Where have you been, fair May Collin ?
　　Who owns this dapple grey ? "
"It is a found one," she replied,
　　"That I got on the way."

Then out bespoke the wily parrot
　　Unto fair May Collin,
"What have you done with false Sir John,
　　That went with you yestreen ? "

"Oh, hold your tongue, my pretty parrot,
　　And talk no more of me ;
And where you had a meal a day,
　　Oh, now you shall have three."

Then up bespoke her father dear,
  From his chamber where he lay,
" What aileth thee, my pretty Poll,
  That you chat so long ere day ? '

" The cat she came to my cage door,
  The thief I could not see,
And I called to fair May Collin
  To take the cat from me."

Then first she told her father dear
  The deed that she had done,
And next she told her mother dear,
  Concerning false Sir John.

" If this be true, fair May Collin,
  That you have told to me,
Before I either eat or drink,
  This false Sir John I'll see."

Away they went with one consent,
  At dawning of the day ;
Until they came to Carline Sands,
  And there his body lay :

His body tall, by that great fall,
  By the waves tossed to and fro,
The diamond ring that he had on,
  Was broke in pieces two.

And they have taken up his corpse
    To yonder pleasant green,
And there they have buried false Sir John,
    For fear he should be seen.*

* This is a much fuller set of the ballad than I ever saw
printed. It is probable that Collin, or Colvin, is a corrup-
tion of Colvill; and that Carline Sands means Carlinseugh
Sands, on the coast of Forfarshire. Sir John's charm
resembles that used by Sir John Colquhoun in 1633, and
the glamour of Faa, the Egyptian, touching whose amorous
adventure and tragical end, I may here mention some
lines expressive of the powers of the husband's family
which I found among the Macfarlane MSS. :—

    " 'Twixt Wigton and the town of Air,
        Portpatrick and the crnives of Crea,
    No man needs think for to bide there,
        Unless he court with Kennedie."

I will only add that May Collin's appropriation of her
lover's steed, though unromantic, may be justified by the
example of the Princess of Cathay herself, and Ariosto in-
forms us that Angelica was never at a loss for a palfrey;
when Orlando had seized one, from which she fell, she
would steal another.—C. K. S.

    The ballad was first published in Mr. Herd's "Ancient
and Modern Scottish Songs" (1769). A third version is
given by Motherwell.

XVIII.
MY MITHER BUILT A WEE, WEE HOUSE.
(*Tune*, " Birks of Abergeldie."*)

My mither built a wee, wee house,
A wee, wee house, a wee, wee house,
My mither built a wee, wee house,
To keep me frae the men, O !
The wa's fell in, and I fell out,
The wa's fell in, and I fell out,
The wa's fell in, and I fell out,
Amang the merry men, O !

How can I keep my maidenhead,
My maidenhead, my maidenhead,
How can I keep my maidenhead,
Amang sae mony men, O ?
Ane auld mouldy maidenhead,
Ane auld mouldy maidenhead,
Ane auld mouldy maidenhead,
Seven years and ten, O !

The captain bad a guinea for 't,
A guinea for 't, a guinea for 't,
The captain bad a guinea for 't,
The colonel he bad ten, O !
The sergeant he bad naething for 't,
Bad naething for 't, bad naething for 't,
The sergeant he bad naething for 't,
And he came farrest ben, O !

---

* *Sic* in original, but "The Birks of *Aberfeldie*" is the
name the tune is best known by.

XIX.

THE TWA BROTHERS.

THERE were twa brethern in the north,
They went to the school* thegither ;
The one unto the other said,
" Will you try a warsle afore?"

They warsled up, they warsled down,
Till Sir John fell to the ground,
And there was a knife in Sir Willie's pouch,
Gied him a deadlie wound.

"Oh, brither, dear, take me on your back,
Carry me to yon burn clear,
And wash the blood from off my wound,
And it will bleed nae mair."

He took him up upon his back,
Carried him to you burn clear,
And wash'd the blood from off his wound,
But aye it bled the mair.

"Oh brither, dear, take me on your back,
Carry me to yon kirk-yard ;
And dig a grave baith wide and deep,
And lay my body there."

---

* Chase is sometimes substituted for school.—C. K. S.

He's ta'en him up upon his back,
Carried him to yon kirk-yard ;
And dug a grave baith deep and wide,
And laid his body there.

"But what will I say to my father dear,
Gin he chance to say, 'Willie, whar's John?'"
"Oh, say that he's to England gone,
To buy him a cask of wine."

"And what will I say to my mother dear,
Gin she chance to say, 'Willie, whar's John?'"
"Oh, say that he's to England gone,
To buy her a new silk gown."

"An' what will I say to my sister dear,
Gin she chance to say, 'Willie, whar's John?'"
"Oh, say that he's to England gone,
To buy her a wedding-ring."

"But what will I say to her you lo'e dear,
Gin she cry, 'Why tarries my John?'"
"Oh, tell her I lie in kirk-land fair,
And home again will never come."*

' In the month of July, 1588, at the Drum, near Dal-
keith, William, Master of Somerville, accidentally killed his
brother John, with whom he had ever lived in the most
affectionate manner, by the unexpected discharge of his
pistol ("Memorie of the Somervilles," vol. i. p. 466). This
event, I am convinced, is the origin of this ballad, of which
a fuller and more correct edition is to be found in Jamieson.
As to kirk-land, my copy has only kirk-yard, till the last
verse, where *land* has been added from conjecture. Kirk-

XX.

THE TWA LASSES.

O BESSIE BELL and Mary Gray,
 They war twa bonnie lasses!
They bigget a bower on yon burn brae,
 And theekit it o'er wi' rashes.

They theekit it o'er wi' rashes green,
 They theekit it o'er with heather,
But the pest cam' frae the burrows town,
 And slew them baith thegither!

They thought to lye in Methven Kirk yard,
 Amang their noble kin,
But they maun lye in Stronach Haugh,
 To biek forenent the sin.
And Bessie Bell and Mary Gray,
 They war twa bonnie lasses!
They biggit a bower on yon burn brae,
 And theekit it o'er wi' rashes.*

END OF PART I.

---

land, or Inchmurry, is in Perthshire.—N.B. A similar
accident happened in the Stair family, 1682.—C. K. S.

 This ballad was first published by Jamieson in his
"Popular Ballads and Songs" (1806). A third version is
given by Motherwell.

 * Bessy Bell and Mary Gray died of the plague, com-
municated by their lover, in the year 1645. Their romantic
history may be found in "Pennant's Tour," and in the
"Statistical Account of Scotland." The more modern words
of this ballad were composed by Allan Ramsay.—C. K. S.